SPORTING 🏆 HEROES

HARRY KANE

ROY APPS

ILLUSTRATED BY ALESSANDRO VALDRIGHI

LONDON • SYDNEY

Franklin Watts
First published in Great Britain in 2018
by The Watts Publishing Group

Text © Roy Apps 2018
Illustrations © Watts Publishing Group 2018
Illustrator: Alessandro Valdrighi
Cover design by Peter Scoulding
Executive Editor: Adrian Cole

*The statistics in this book were correct at the time
of printing, but because of the nature of the sport,
it cannot be guaranteed that they are now accurate.*

HB ISBN 978 1 4451 5212 7
PB ISBN 978 1 4451 5213 4
Library ebook ISBN 978 1 4451 5215 8

1 3 5 7 9 10 8 6 4 2

Printed in China

MIX
Paper from
responsible sources
FSC® C104740
FSC
www.fsc.org

CHAPTER TWO
SCOUTED BY...

No one believed Harry and his mates when they said they'd had a kick around with the England and Tottenham Hotspur striker, Jermain Defoe.

Harry carried on playing for Ridgeway Rovers. There were always scouts from professional clubs having a look at the various boys' and youth squads. That's how Harry had got to play for Arsenal as an eight-year-old, before eventually going back to Ridgeway.

To tell the truth, he hadn't been that bothered when his playing days with Arsenal had come to an end after just a year. He'd only been a kid, after all. Now, though, he was in Year 7. Older students were already beginning to talk about what job they wanted to do when they left school. Harry wondered if he'd ever get another chance to become a professional footballer.

One Saturday afternoon, just as Harry and his dad were leaving the ground, the club chairman called out to them: 'Harry! Pat! Have you got a moment?'

Harry and his dad waited for the chairman to catch up to them.

'We had a couple of scouts in this afternoon. One of them is interested in Harry doing some training with his club to see how he gets on.'

'Which club would that be?' asked Harry's dad.

Harry hoped it would be one of the big London teams: Chelsea, West Ham United — or even the club his family had supported for as long as he could remember, Jermain Defoe's club, Spurs.

'Watford,' the chairman replied.

CHAPTER THREE
COME ON, YOU SPURS!

In 2004, Harry started doing some training sessions with Watford Football Club, who were playing in the Championship, one division below the Premier League. He'd been at Watford for a couple of months, when he and his dad were called over to see the youth coach at the end of one training session.

'Harry! Pat! Come over.'

Harry strolled over with his dad. As he got closer, Harry saw that the youth coach's expression was serious. Harry knew that look. He'd seen it on the face of the Arsenal schoolboy coach when Harry had been told he was no longer wanted at the club.

A Spurs fan? Harry had been a Spurs fan since the day he was born. Even when he had been at Arsenal as an eight-year-old, he would've played in his blue-and-white Spurs kit, rather than the red of Arsenal, if he'd thought he could've got away with it.

'I thought you'd want to get over to White Hart Lane as soon as possible,' said the coach. He shook Harry's hand. 'All the best, Harry. I only hope we don't ever find ourselves playing Spurs with you in their squad.'

Harry loved being at the Spurs academy. Sometimes, he'd see Jermain Defoe at the training ground.

Best of all though were the Spurs' home games. Harry went to as many as he could, watching Jermain Defoe scoring goal after goal. One day, he thought, I could be out there on the pitch playing for the first team.

CHAPTER FOUR
FIRST-TEAM FOOTBALL

Harry progressed through the academy at Spurs. During the 2009—10 season, as a 16-year-old, he played 22 matches for Spurs' Under-18s team. He scored an impressive 18 goals. At the end of the season, he signed his first professional contract with the club.

He was a proper Spurs player now. It was just that it didn't really feel like it. A match every other week for the reserves was the sum total of the football he was playing.

His mum sensed his frustration. 'Harry, you're only 17! Just be patient.'

'But I want to be playing more games! I want to score goals!'

One day in early January 2011, one of the reserve team coaches took him aside. 'Harry, you need to be playing more games.'

'At last! Someone who agrees with me!' said Harry.

'We'd like to send you out on loan for the rest of the season. To Leyton Orient. It'll mean first-team football for you.'

Leyton Orient played in League One and were just down the road from Harry's home in Chingford.

Straightaway, he liked it at Orient. It was a friendly place.

'Harry,' said Russell Slade, the manager, 'let me introduce you to our winger, Dean Cox. He's new to the club, too. I think you two could work well together.'

Harry took one look at Dean and frowned. The winger was short — only 1.63m. Harry was over 1.88m.

'Dean delivers a mean cross. And Harry, I've already seen your heading skills on the training pitch,' explained Russell Slade.

Harry practised set pieces with Dean during training. Russell Slade watched them.

'Harry, you'll be in the starting 11 this Saturday. We're at home to Sheffield Wednesday.'

LEYTON ORIENT VS
SHEFFIELD WEDNESDAY.
57TH MINUTE.

ORIENT HAVE A FREE
KICK WITHIN RANGE...

DEAN COX SETS
THE BALL DOWN.

CHAPTER FIVE
ON THE ROAD AGAIN

Harry went on to score another four goals for Orient. He returned to Spurs for the start of the 2011–12 season. Having been playing first-team football every week, he felt like he was now a proper professional. He knew there was still a long way to go though. The first team included Jermain Defoe and Gareth Bale, so it would be a while before he could challenge for a place.

August saw the qualification matches for the UEFA Europa League. Spurs won the first leg of their match against the Scottish side Hearts 5–0.

'Harry, the gaffer's keen to make some changes for the second leg,' the reserve team coach told him. 'Letting some of the youngsters get some match time — including you.'

When Harry went in to check the team sheet for the match, his name was on the list. He stood, frozen to the spot. He was in the starting lineup!

The Spurs youngsters made a lively start. The match was only into its 28th minute when Harry Kane tore into the box, the ball at his feet. The Hearts goalkeeper stuck out a leg and the young striker came crashing down.

'Penalty!'

Harry stepped up to take the spot kick. This could be the biggest moment in his life: his first goal for Spurs.

He struck the ball sweetly and it thundered towards the goal. The Hearts keeper was equal to it though and produced a smart save. Harry clutched his head in horror.

The young striker was devastated.

'Awwww...' groaned the Spurs supporters.

Just after Christmas, Harry and his teammate Ryan Mason were called into the manager Harry Redknapp's office:

'Harry, Ryan, you boys have both done well. But you're still some way off getting into the first-team squad. So, I'm sending you out on loan — to Millwall.'

Harry Kane was off on the road again.

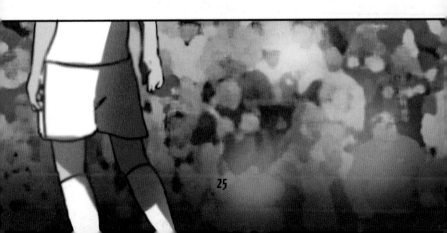

CHAPTER SIX
WARMING THE BENCH

Harry enjoyed his time at Millwall. After a slow start, he began to score goals regularly. At the end of the 2012–2013 season, he was named Millwall's Young Player of the Year.

He returned to Spurs to find the club had a new manager, André Villas-Boas, who had his own plans for the development of the first-team squad: Harry wasn't part of them.

'We're sending you out on loan again, Harry.'

'Where to this time?'

'Norwich City.'

'It could be worse,' Harry thought.
'At least they're a Premiership Club
— and their manager knows me.' The
Norwich manager, Chris Hughton, had
once been Spurs' assistant manager
and knew Harry well.

Harry's second match in Norwich
colours was a League Cup tie against
Doncaster Rovers. Harry was excited.
At last it all seemed to be coming
together. He was getting regular
matches in a Premiership team under
a manager he knew.

He was desperate to make a good
impression. He didn't do a lot in the
first 45 minutes, but just after the
break, he picked up the ball in his own
half and ran hard at the Doncaster
central defence. He looked up, and saw
that he still had to get past their full
back. Harry spun on his heel to make a
quick turn — too quick!

'Aargh!'

He felt his ankle give way. He crashed painfully to the ground. Moments later, the Norwich medical team were at his side.

Harry had broken a bone in his foot. It would be at least six weeks before he'd be able to play again.

'He'll be a big loss because he is a young player of fabulous potential that we brought in for a specific reason,' the Norwich manager, Chris Hughton said. 'I feel for him at the moment.'

The following February, back at Spurs and fully recovered from his injury, Harry was called into the manager's office again.

BUT HARRY MADE JUST FIVE STARTS FOR LEICESTER.

HARRY SPENT A LOT OF TIME WARMING THE SUBS' BENCH...
SITTING NEXT TO ANOTHER PLAYER THE STAFF DIDN'T SEEM KEEN TO PLAY: JAMIE VARDY.
I'M THINKING OF PUTTING IN A TRANSFER REQUEST AT THE END OF THE SEASON.
WHAT ABOUT YOU, HARRY? ARE YOU GOING TO HANG AROUND AT SPURS?
I'M SPURS THROUGH AND THROUGH. I DON'T WANT TO PLAY FOR ANYONE ELSE. BUT I REALLY DON'T KNOW WHAT'S GOING TO HAPPEN...

CHAPTER SEVEN
THE NUMBER 18 SHIRT

At the start of the 2013—2014 season, Harry was called in to see the Spurs manager.

'Leicester want you back on loan,' he said.

Harry groaned.

'But you're not going anywhere,' the manager continued. 'I'm not having you going back to Leicester to spend match days warming your bum on the subs' bench. You're staying put.'

A few weeks later, though, for the League Cup match against Hull, Harry found himself on the subs' bench again.

'At least it's the Spurs subs' bench,'
he thought to himself.

Then, the manager turned to him.
'Harry! Get yourself warmed up. You're
going on.'

It was late in the match and it was
1–1. Harry got quickly into his stride,
but there was no way through the Hull
defence. The ref blew for extra time.

Nine minutes into extra time, and Spurs found themselves a goal down. Three minutes into the second period of extra time, Harry popped up from nowhere and drilled a low shot straight towards the far corner of the Hull goal.

'GOAL!'

The home crowd went wild! So did Harry. It was his first goal at White Hart Lane.

Harry felt an arm round his shoulder.

'Told you you'd got a good first touch, Harry!'

It was his hero — now his teammate — Jermain Defoe.

The home crowd urged their team on, but Spurs just couldn't get the winner. The game went to penalties. Harry sighed. As a life-time Spurs fan, he knew his team's record when it came to penalty shootouts: it was rubbish! The last penalty shootout they had won had been back in 1994, when he'd been just a few months old.

The first three penalty kicks from both sides all went in. It came to Harry's turn. He placed the ball on the spot. The crowd fell silent. A short run up, then Harry's thunderous shot sailed past the Hull keeper.

Spurs won the penalty shootout 8–7 to book their place in the next round of the League Cup.

At the end of the January 2014 transfer window, the news that everybody in the Spurs' dressing room had been whispering about was finally confirmed.

SPURS SELL DEFOE TO TORONTO FOR £6 MILLION!

The Spurs team met up on the training ground to say goodbye to the legendary striker. In his hand, Jermain Defoe held the famous Spurs number 18 shirt he had worn during his time at the club.

'There are goals to be scored in this shirt,' he told the squad. 'And I'd like to hand it on to a young player who I first kicked a ball with many years ago on the streets of Chingford. Harry Kane, you are the new Spurs number 18!'

For a moment, Harry just stood there, unable to move. He'd always known he was a Spurs player, through and through. Now, with Jermain Defoe's number 18 shirt in his possession, he was ready to start another chapter in his footballing career.

CHAPTER EIGHT
ONE OF OUR OWN

The date: Saturday 7th February 2015.
The match: Spurs vs Arsenal, better
known as the North London Derby.

There were still more than three
months left of the season, but Harry
Kane had already scored twenty goals.
What could he do in this most famous
of football fixtures?

If the first half was anything to go
by, not a lot. Spurs came up against
a solid and stubborn Arsenal defence.
When the teams went off at half time,
Arsenal led 1—0.

In the 56th minute, Spurs won a corner.
The ball drifted high into the box; a
flick from Mousa Dembélé and Harry

stabbed it into the back of the net: 1—1!

'Y-e-e-e-s-s-s-s!'

Four minutes from the full-time whistle and it was still 1—1. On the left wing, Nabil Bentaleb curled a high ball towards the Arsenal goal. Harry met it with his head and powered a shot into the top left-hand corner: 2—1 to Spurs!

A new chant began to be heard echoing loudly around the Spurs' home end:

'He's one of our own, he's one of our own, Harry Kane, he's one of our own!'

Harry Kane, the boy who had once played football in the street with his hero Jermain Defoe, was himself now well on his way to becoming a Spurs sporting legend.

SPORTING 🏆 HEROES

FACT FILE

Full name: Harry Edward Kane

Date of birth: 28th July 1993

Place of birth: Walthamstow, Greater London

Height: 1.88m (6ft 2in)

Club: Tottenham Hotspur

GLOSSARY

academy — youth football training school, with professional coaches and facilities, often linked to a particular club

autograph — signature of a famous sports star or celebrity

geezers — slang word used in London to describe men

loaned out — sent to play for another team for a set period of time

promotion — move up from a lower division in a league

scout — someone who looks for talented football players

White Hart Lane — home ground of Spurs in north London

winger — football playing position on the extreme edge of the pitch, known as the wing

CAREER

Youth Career:

Ridgeway Rovers	1999—2001
Arsenal	2001—2002
Ridgeway Rovers	2002—2004
Watford	2004
Tottenham Hotspur (Spurs)	2004—2009

Senior Career:

Tottenham Hotspur	2009—
— loaned to Leyton Orient	2011
— loaned to Millwall	2012
— loaned to Norwich City	2012—2013
— loaned to Leicester City	2013

England International record:

Under 17 — 3 appearances, 2 goals
Under 19 — 14 appearances, 6 goals
Under 20 — 3 appearances, 1 goal
Under 21 — 14 appearances, 8 goals
England senior team debut - 19 March 2015

Honours:

Millwall Young Player of the Season	2011—2012
PFA Young Player of the Year	2014—2015
Spurs' highest goalscorer in a single season	2014—2015
Tottenham Hotspur Player of the Year	2014—2015
Premier League Golden Boot	2015—2016, 2016—2017
Premier League Player of the Month	Jan 2015, Feb 2015, Mar 2016, Feb 2017, Sep 2017
PFA Fans' Premier League Player of the Season	2016—17
Premier League PFA Team of the Year	2014—2015, 2015—2016, 2016—2017

It was scary. Lonely. On the streets at night. There were noises everywhere. Cars and taxis hooting, buses revving, people calling out and shouting.

One night, while Fara was curled up under the arches down by the river, an old guy came and sat down beside her... He looked hard at the football boots Fara was clutching.

'Nice boots. Do you play?'

Fara nodded. 'For Chelsea Ladies...'

CONTINUE READING
FARA'S
AMAZING STORY IN...

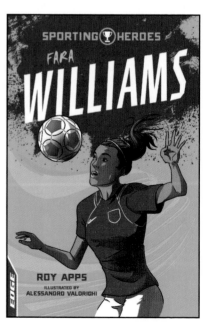